Norwegian Americans

Nichol Bryan

ABDO
Publishing Company

Norwegian Americans

Europeans first sailed to the New World in 1492. Part of the New World eventually became America, a nation of **immigrants**. For hundreds of years after the first Europeans arrived, people from around the world made the long voyage to America.

These immigrants made the journey for many different reasons. Some fled the rule of **dictators**. Many looked for a place to safely practice their religion. Others wanted to escape poverty.

Escaping poverty was a major reason immigrants came from Norway to the United States. They came so their children would have more opportunities. Often, one or two members of a family would come first. In letters home, they encouraged their families to follow.

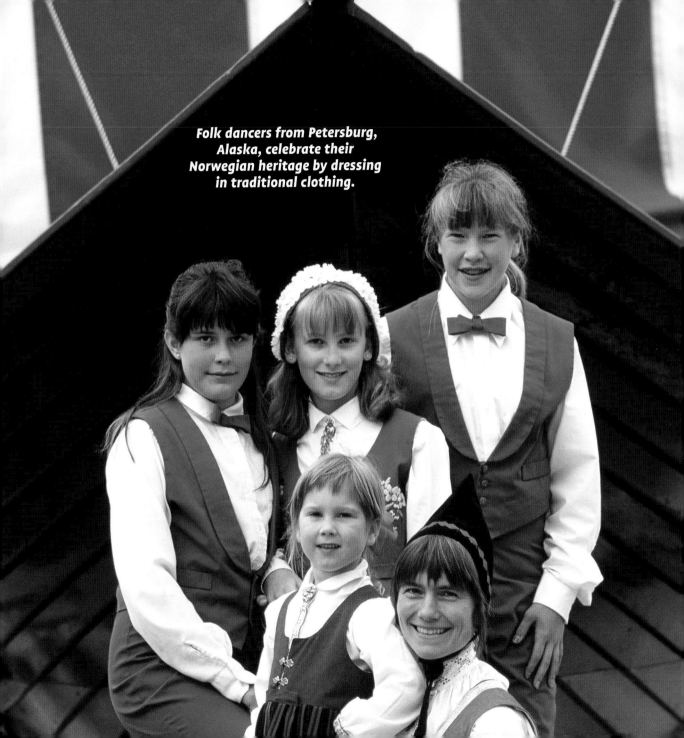

Folk dancers from Petersburg, Alaska, celebrate their Norwegian heritage by dressing in traditional clothing.

Northern Land

Norway is in northern Europe. It is a land of mountain ranges, glaciers, and **fjords**. Farmland is scarce. Towns are sometimes separated by impassable peaks and dense forests.

More than 12,000 years ago, much of this area was covered with ice. But, hunters and fishers still made this land their home. Around 3000 BC, these ancient peoples began to farm and keep livestock. By AD 100, Germanic tribes had moved into the region and formed small kingdoms.

Around 800, warlike Norwegians known as Vikings began sailing the seas. They built mighty warships and conquered surrounding lands. Wherever they went, the Vikings conquered native peoples and hauled away food, slaves, and treasure. They settled in England, Ireland, and Iceland.

Around this time, a powerful king called Harald I Fairhair brought many of Norway's kingdoms under his control. Several kings after him continued to bring the country under a central royal power.

Rivers and glaciers created the fjords of Norway.

The prospect of plentiful, inexpensive land seemed too good to be true. But, these **immigrants** faced harsh winters and loneliness on the wide prairies. A typical home for these settlers was a log house. Sometimes, the roof was made of **sod**, straw, or hay.

Many Norwegians had an easier time in the Pacific Northwest. They settled near thick forests. These surroundings reminded them of home. Some became loggers or fishers. Norwegian sailors found they could earn more money on American ships. And, laborers were able to find work in the cities.

A Norwegian immigrant sits by her sod house in Minnesota around 1896.

Norwegian-American Communities

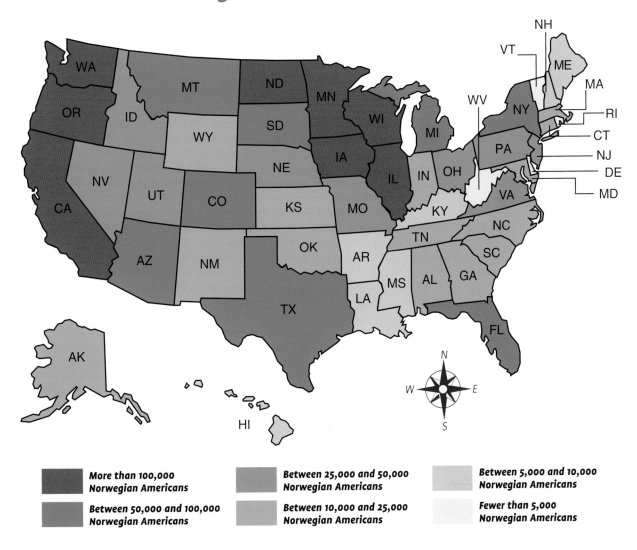

Legend:

- **More than 100,000 Norwegian Americans**
- **Between 50,000 and 100,000 Norwegian Americans**
- **Between 25,000 and 50,000 Norwegian Americans**
- **Between 10,000 and 25,000 Norwegian Americans**
- **Between 5,000 and 10,000 Norwegian Americans**
- **Fewer than 5,000 Norwegian Americans**

As they settled, Norwegians formed communities with other Norwegians. Often, they lived with people from their former towns or villages in Norway. This helped Norwegians keep much of their language and **culture** alive. Norwegians also formed their own churches and schools.

Norwegian immigrants modeled some buildings, such as the Norway Building in Wisconsin, after Norwegian churches.

Norwegian **immigrants** did not face some of the **discrimination** that many other immigrants did. This was because most of them were white Protestants. But, there was some pressure to become more American. So, the children of the first Norwegian immigrants quickly adopted the ways of their new country.

As the first Norwegians were settling in America, more arrived. A small wave of Norwegians came to America in the 1920s. However, **quota** laws and the **Great Depression** soon decreased immigration to the United States. But, Norwegian Americans had already become one of the largest **ethnic** groups in America.

Second- and third-generation Norwegian Americans increasingly moved away from their farming and manufacturing jobs. Many attended colleges founded in Norwegian-American communities in the Midwest.

Norwegian Americans now work in all areas of the economy. They work in service jobs, high-tech professions, and management positions. Today, about 4 million Americans claim Norwegian ancestry. That's almost equal to the population of Norway itself!

Becoming a Citizen

Norwegians and other **immigrants** who come to the United States take the same path to citizenship. Immigrants become citizens in a process called naturalization. A government agency called the United States Citizenship and Immigration Services (USCIS) oversees this process.

The Path to Citizenship

Applying for Citizenship

The first step in becoming a citizen is filling out a form. It is called the Application for Naturalization. On the application, immigrants provide information about their past. Immigrants send the application to the USCIS.

Providing Information

Besides the application, immigrants must provide the USCIS with other items. They may include documents such as marriage licenses or old tax returns. Immigrants must also provide photographs and fingerprints. They are used for identification. The fingerprints are also used to check whether immigrants have committed crimes in the past.

The Interview

Next, a USCIS officer interviews each immigrant to discuss his or her application and background. In addition, the USCIS officer tests the immigrant's ability to speak, read, and write in English. The officer also tests the immigrant's knowledge of American civics.

The Oath

Immigrants approved for citizenship must take the Oath of Allegiance. Once immigrants take this oath, they are citizens. During the oath, immigrants promise to renounce loyalty to their native country, to support the U.S. Constitution, and to serve and defend the United States when needed.

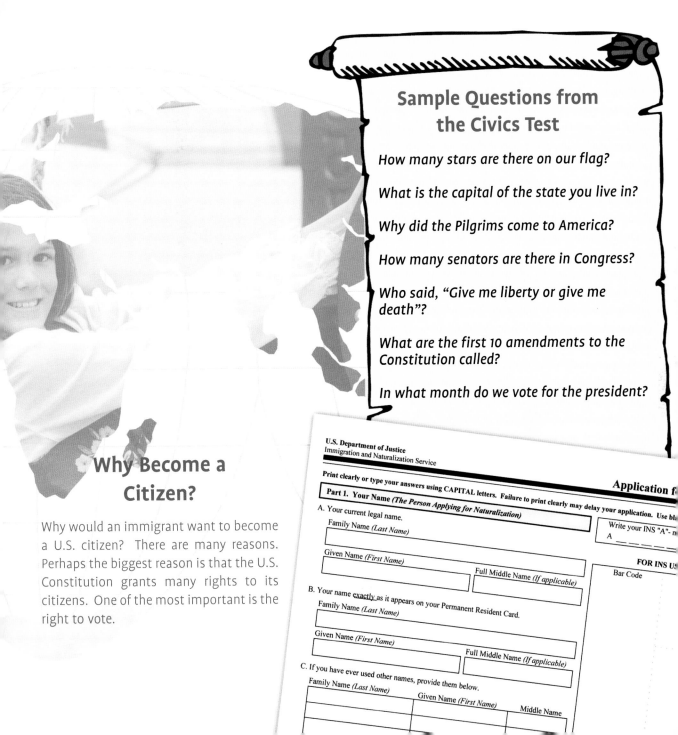

Sample Questions from the Civics Test

How many stars are there on our flag?

What is the capital of the state you live in?

Why did the Pilgrims come to America?

How many senators are there in Congress?

Who said, "Give me liberty or give me death"?

What are the first 10 amendments to the Constitution called?

In what month do we vote for the president?

Why Become a Citizen?

Why would an immigrant want to become a U.S. citizen? There are many reasons. Perhaps the biggest reason is that the U.S. Constitution grants many rights to its citizens. One of the most important is the right to vote.

U.S. Department of Justice
Immigration and Naturalization Service

Print clearly or type your answers using CAPITAL letters. Failure to print clearly may delay your application. Use bla

Application f

Part 1. Your Name *(The Person Applying for Naturalization)*

A. Your current legal name.

Family Name *(Last Name)*

Write your INS "A"- n
A _ _ _ _ _ _

Given Name *(First Name)*

FOR INS US

Full Middle Name *(If applicable)*

Bar Code

B. Your name exactly as it appears on your Permanent Resident Card.

Family Name *(Last Name)*

Given Name *(First Name)*

Full Middle Name *(If applicable)*

C. If you have ever used other names, provide them below.

Family Name *(Last Name)* | Given Name *(First Name)* | Middle Name

Traditions

Many Norwegian Americans have never been to Norway. However, their **heritage** is still important to them. Norwegian traditions, religion, and language are still strong among Norwegian Americans.

Family

The family has always been very important in Norwegian **culture**. In Norway, the eldest son of a farmer inherited the farm. Because of this, Norwegian families traditionally lived together for generations. Family members shared a bond with each other and with their land.

This practice of extended families living together continued in America. However, families were no longer forced to live on the family farm. That's because land was more available in the United States. Many Norwegian-American families grew smaller and moved to cities.

In addition to Syttende Mai, Norwegian Americans also celebrate Norwegian American Day. They often hold parades, such as this one in Boston.

Remembering Norway

Many Norwegian Americans celebrate their Norwegian **heritage** on *Syttende Mai*, or **Constitution** Day. This is the date in 1814 when Norway became free from Danish rule. Norwegian Americans mark *Syttende Mai* with parades, dances, costumes, songs, and food.

Art

Rosemaling is a traditional Norwegian art still practiced by Norwegian Americans today. Plaques, plates, boxes, trunks, and even pieces of furniture are hand-painted with colorful and detailed floral designs. Rosemaling has become a popular hobby for many Norwegian Americans.

Rosemaling can be found in the homes of many Norwegian Americans. This Norwegian-made dresser displays rosemaling on its doors and sides.

A Taste of the Past

Norwegian-American recipes often reflect inexpensive traditions from rural Norway. For instance, lutefisk is one of the most famous Norwegian dishes. It is codfish preserved in lye.

Another popular Norwegian dish, lefse, is a soft flat bread. It is made of potatoes and is often served with butter and sugar. Today, many Norwegian Americans enjoy going to lutefisk and lefse dinners. It reminds them of the simple pleasures of their **immigrant** ancestors.

A grandmother bakes Norwegian cookies for a Norwegian-American festival in North Dakota.

21

A Lasting Faith

King Olaf I Tryggvason converted many Norwegians to Christianity when he took the throne of Norway in 995. Since 1537, the Evangelical Lutheran Church has been the state church of Norway. So, many Norwegian **immigrants** are Lutheran.

Norwegians formed new branches of Lutheranism in their new home. Some of these branches are similar to the Evangelical Lutheran Church of Norway. Some, however, hold different beliefs. Many Norwegian Americans follow other faiths or are not religious. For many Norwegian Americans, however, faith is an important part of their lives.

King Harald V and Queen Sonja of Norway visit a Norwegian church in New York City in 2002.

Language from Another Land

Norway's early language was Old Norse. After Norway united with Denmark, a new form of Norwegian developed called Bokmål. This language uses much of the vocabulary and spelling of Danish. However, Norwegians may also speak Nynorsk, a form of Norwegian that is less Danish.

In large Norwegian-American communities, Norwegian has remained an important language for generations. But over time, many Norwegian **immigrants** learned English in order to get higher-paying jobs. So, few Norwegian Americans can speak Norwegian today. But, many are learning the language of their ancestors.

Norwegians around the world work to preserve their language. This Norwegian woman sells Norwegian-language newspapers in Spain.

23

Contributions

The Norwegian people are known for their belief in hard work. They are also known for their love of the arts and learning. Norwegian Americans have built on this **heritage**. They have succeeded in American literature and art, as well as in science, industry, and sports.

One Norwegian **immigrant** who became an important American novelist is Ole Rölvaag. He came to the United States in 1896. His novels *Giants in the Earth*, *Peder Victorious,* and *Their Fathers' God* are moving portrayals of immigrant life.

Another Norwegian-American writer, Robert Bly, was born in Minnesota. He studied at St. Olaf College for a year before moving on to Harvard University. He became one of America's most respected poets.

Norwegian Americans have also been successful in business. Ole Evinrude settled in Cambridge, Wisconsin, with his family in 1882. He invented and patented the first **outboard motor** in 1911.

Robert Bly

Evinrude then founded **Outboard** Marine Corporation, or OMC. It grew to become one of the world's leading producers of outboard motors.

Norwegian Americans have also succeeded in politics. Hubert H. Humphrey was born in Wallace, South Dakota. He moved to Minnesota and eventually became mayor of Minneapolis, and later a U.S. senator. He became vice president under Lyndon B. Johnson in 1965.

Another Norwegian-American vice president, Walter Mondale, was born in Ceylon, Minnesota. He helped in Humphrey's Senate campaign. Mondale became a U.S. senator in 1964. In 1976, Mondale was elected vice president under Jimmy Carter.

Hubert H. Humphrey

Ivar Giaever works in his lab in 1966.

Some Norwegian Americans have won the Nobel Prize, including many in the field of science. One of these people, Ivar Giaever, was born in Norway. In 1954, he moved to Canada. He then moved to New York in 1956, where he became more interested in physics. He received his **PhD** in 1964.

Giaever won the Nobel Prize in Physics in 1973. He shared the prize with two other scientists. Giaever was honored with the prize for his work in **superconductivity**. One of the many Norwegian Americans to succeed in science, Giaever is a role model to all Norwegian **immigrants**.

Another Norwegian-American Nobel Prize winner is Ernest O. Lawrence. He was born in South Dakota to Norwegian **immigrants**. He earned his **PhD** in chemistry at Yale University in 1925. Fourteen years later, he won the Nobel Prize in Physics for inventing a device called the cyclotron. It speeds up the movement of atoms.

Many Norwegian Americans have also won fame in the world of sports. However, few are more important than Babe Didrikson. The daughter of Norwegian Americans, she was born in Port Arthur, Texas, in 1911. She took an interest in sports at a time when girls were discouraged from being athletic.

Didrikson was a star basketball player in high school. In the 1932 Olympic Games, she was a gold medalist in track and field. She then switched to golf and became a national sensation, winning many tournaments. Didrikson was named Associated Press Woman Athlete of the Year six times! She showed American women that they could be successful athletes.

The Viking explorers probably never dreamed their descendants would come to North America in such large numbers. Norwegian Americans played a vital role in building the United States. Today, their descendants are successful Americans who are proud of their **heritage**.

Babe Didrikson tees up at the Weathervane Tournament in Miami Beach, Florida, in 1952. She was a founding member of the Ladies Professional Golf Association.

Glossary

constitution - the laws that govern a country.

culture - the customs, arts, and tools of a nation or people at a certain time.

dictator - a ruler with complete control who usually governs in a cruel or unfair way.

discrimination - unfair treatment based on factors such as a person's race, religion, or gender.

ethnic - of or having to do with a group of people who are of the same race, nationality, or culture.

fjord - a long, narrow, and deep inlet of a sea between two steep slopes.

Great Depression - a period (from 1929 to 1942) of worldwide economic trouble when there was little buying or selling, and many people could not find work.

heritage - the handing down of something from one generation to the next.

immigration - entry into another country to live. A person who immigrates is called an immigrant.

outboard motor - an engine attached to the outside of a boat.

PhD - doctor of philosophy, a degree earned by students who have studied for a number of years in a certain subject.

quota - a limit to the number of people allowed to immigrate in a year.

social democracy - a political and economic system in which the government controls some of the distribution of goods and services. The people elect officials to represent them in the government.

sod - a rectangular section of grass held together by roots.

superconductivity - a material's loss of resistance to the flow of electricity.

Saying It

Bokmål - BOOK-mawl
fjord - fee-AWRD
Ivar Giaever - EE-vahr YAE-vuhr
lefse - LEHF-suh
Leif Eriksson - LAVE EHR-ihk-suhn
lutefisk - LOOT-fisk
Olaf Tryggvason - OH-lawv trig-VAH-sah
Ole Rölvaag - OH-luh ROHL-vahg
rosemaling - ROH-zuh-mah-ling
Syttende Mai - siht-NAH MYE

Web Sites

To learn more about Norwegian Americans, visit ABDO Publishing Company on the World Wide Web at **www.abdopub.com**. Web sites about Norwegian Americans are featured on our Book Links page. These links are routinely monitored and updated to provide the most current information available.

Index